AT THE SIGN OF THE LION
AND OTHER ESSAYS

Now style is something far more than the possession of a rich vocabulary or a keen ear for rhythm and melody; it is primarily an intellectual quality. The first requisite of a good style is that the writer should have a clear vision of his subject, and firmly grasp the logical interrelation of its parts. It is on this basis that the admirable styles of Macaulay, Huxley, and Mill are built. When to this is added a keen perception of the emotional colour of words, you get the really great styles of Newman and Ruskin. Without putting Mr. Belloc on a level with either of the latter, I venture to maintain that he combines in a higher degree than any writer of the day these two fundamental elements of distinction in style.

BURNELL PAYNE.

AT THE SIGN OF THE LION
AND OTHER ESSAYS FROM THE BOOKS OF HILAIRE BELLOC

Essay Index Reprint Series

BOOKS FOR LIBRARIES PRESS
FREEPORT, NEW YORK

First Published 1916
Reprinted in this Series 1964, 1969

STANDARD BOOK NUMBER:
8369-1318-3

LIBRARY OF CONGRESS CATALOG CARD NUMBER:
67-22071

PRINTED IN THE UNITED STATES OF AMERICA

CONTENTS

	PAGE
FOREWORD	vii
AT THE SIGN OF THE LION .	3
THE AUTUMN AND THE FALL OF LEAVES	23
ON SACRAMENTAL THINGS . .	31
ON REST	46
ON COMING TO AN END . .	55

FOREWORD

IN *reprinting these five essays from the works of Hilaire Belloc I believe my readers will find what I have found, that he is both wonder and wild desire when you come to know him at his best.*[1] *I have already cited Mr. Burnell Payne, and I cannot do better than enlarge my quotation: "How widely read Mr. Belloc's books may be I do not know, but there is no*

---

[1] *The Four Men: a Farrago,* so called by its author, is a book that, speaking for myself as well as for others who have read it, puts forth a perfect flowering in speech and song. You enter an enchanted country, meeting its true citizens who will remain with you in humour and in pathos and in all the wonderful things that go to make up a journey of divine adventure.

*doubt that on those who do read them
they exert a very powerful influence;
and the secret of this influence lies,
more than anything else, in their
style."*

*A more recent critic, Mr. Thomas
Seccombe, who is already known by an
enduring Introduction to the works
of George Gissing, has still further
enlarged the boundaries of our knowledge of Belloc and his books. I am glad
to point out that this delightful study
can be found in* The Living Age *for
April 8, 1916; as also Mr. Payne's
appreciation, a few months earlier. If
I did not succeed in making it clear
that Hilaire Belloc is a poet as well as
writer of unexcelled prose, I should feel
I had neglected a solemn obligation. It
is when the singing soul of our author is*
in excelsis *that we get exquisite things
from the least expected sources. In a*

FOREWORD

Dedicatory Ode *of most excellent fooling we find stanzas like these:*

"They say that in the unchanging place,
 Where all we loved is always dear,
We meet our morning face to face
 And find at last our twentieth year . . . .

They say (and I am glad they say)
 It is so; and it may be so:
It may be just the other way,
 I cannot tell. But this I know:

From quiet homes and first beginning,
 Out to the undiscovered ends,
There's nothing worth the wear of winning,
 But laughter and the love of friends.

Then consider from the same poem, as noted by Mr. Seccombe, "a beautiful Tennysonian passage about the Evenlode:"

" The quiet evening kept her tryst:
 Beneath an open sky we rode,
And passed into a wandering mist
 Along the perfect Evenlode.

ix

FOREWORD

The tender Evenlode that makes
  Her meadows hush to hear the sound
Of waters mingling in the brakes,
  And binds my heart to English ground.

A lovely river, all alone,
  She lingers in the hills and holds
A hundred little towns of stones,
  Forgotten in the western wolds."

Why do I make mention of these poetic perfections? Because I love them, and I want to render unto Belloc the things that are his and have also become mine in that I sought and found them. Let me reiterate a final appreciation: " as an essayist he already occupies one of the very first places in English Literature."

T. B. M.

AT THE SIGN OF THE LION
AND OTHER ESSAYS

AT THE SIGN OF THE LION

IT was late, and the day was already falling when I came, sitting my horse Monster, to a rise of land. We were at a walk, for we had gone very far since early morning, and were now off the turf upon the hard road; moreover, the hill, though gentle, had been prolonged. From its summit I saw before me, as I had seen it a hundred times, the whole of the weald.

But now that landscape was transfigured, because many influences had met to make it, for the moment, an enchanted land. The autumn, coming late, had crowded it with colours; a slight mist drew out the distances, and along the horizon stood out, quite even and grey like mountains, the solemn presence of the Downs. Over all this the sky was full of storm.

In some manner which language cannot express, and hardly music, the vision was unearthly. All the lesser heights of the plain ministered to one effect, a picture which was to other pictures what the marvellous is to the experience of common things. The distant mills, the edges of heath and the pine trees, were as though they had not before been caught by the eyes of travellers, and would not, after the brief space of their apparition, be seen again. Here was a countryside whose every outline was familiar; and yet it was pervaded by a general quality of the uplifted and the strange. And for that one hour under the sunset the county did not

4

seem to me a thing well known, but rather adored.

The glow of evening, which had seemed to put this horizon into another place and time than ours, warned me of darkness; and I made off the road to the right for an inn I knew of, that stands close to the upper Arun and is very good. Here an old man and his wife live easily, and have so lived for at least thirty years, proving how accessible is content. Their children are in service beyond the boundaries of the county, and are thus provided with sufficiency; and they themselves, the old people, enjoy a small possession which at least does not diminish, for, thank God, their land is free. It is a square of pasture bordered by great elms upon three sides of it, but on the fourth, towards the water, a line of pollard willows; and off a little way before the house runs Arun, sliding as smooth as Mincius, and still so young that he can remember the lake in the forest where he rose.

On such ancestral land these two people await without anxiety what they believe will be a kindly death. Nor is their piety of that violent and tortured kind which is associated with fear and with distress of earlier life; but they remain peasants, drawing from the earth they have always known as much sustenance for the soul as even their religion can afford them, and mixing that religion so intimately with their experience of the soil that, were they not isolated in an evil time, they would have set up some shrine about the place to sanctify it.

The passion and the strain which

6

must accompany (even in the happiest and most secluded) the working years of life, have so far disappeared from them, that now they can no longer recall any circumstances other than those which they enjoy; so that their presence in a room about one, as they set food before one or meet one at the door, is in itself an influence of peace.

In such a place, and with such hosts to serve him, the wears of the world retire for a little time, from an evening to a morning; and a man can enjoy a great refreshment. In such a place he will eat strongly and drink largely, and sleep well and deeply, and, when he saddles again for his journey, he will take the whole world new; nor are those intervals without their future value, for the memory of a complete repose is a sort of sacrament, and a viaticum for the weary lengths of the way.

The stable of this place is made of oak entirely, and, after more than a hundred years, the woodwork is still sound, save that the roof now falls in waves where the great beams have sagged a little under the pressure of the tiles. And these tiles are of that old handmade kind which, whenever you find them, you will do well to buy; for they have a slight downward curve to them, and so they fit closer and shed the rain better than if they were flat. Also they do not slip, and thus they put less strain upon the timber. This excellent stable has no flooring but a packed layer of chalk laid on the ground; and the wooden manger is all polished and shining, where it has been rubbed by the noses of ten thousand horses since the great war.

That polishing was helped, perhaps, by the nose of Percy's horse, and perhaps by the nose of some wheeler who in his time had dragged the guns back aboard, retreating through the night after Corunna. It is in every way a stable that a small peasant should put up for himself, without seeking money from other men. It is, therefore, a stable which your gaping scientists would condemn; and though as yet they have not got their ugly hands upon the dwellings of beasts as they have upon those of men, yet I often fear for this stable, and am always glad when I come back and find it there. For the men who make our laws are the same as those that sell us our bricks and our land and our metals; and they make the laws so that rebuilding shall go on: and vile rebuilding too.

Anyhow, this stable yet stands; and in none does the horse, Monster, take a greater delight, for he also is open to the influence of holiness. So I led him in, and tied him by the ancient headstall, and I rubbed him down, and I washed his feet and covered him with the rough rug that lay there. And when I had done all that, I got him oats from the neighbouring bin; for the place knew me well, and I could always tend to my own beast when I came there. And as he ate his oats, I said to him: "Monster, my horse, is there any place on earth where a man, even for a little time, can be as happy as the brutes? If there is, it is here at the Sign of The Lion." And Monster answered: "There is a tradition among us that, of all creatures that creep upon the earth, man is the fullest of sorrow."

I left him then, and went towards the house. It was quite dark, and the windows, with their square, large panes and true proportions, shone out and made it home. The room within received me like a friend. The open chimney at its end, round which the house is built, was filled with beech logs burning; and the candles, which were set in brass, mixed their yellow light with that of the fire. The long ceiling was low, as are the ceilings of Heaven. And oak was here everywhere also: in the beams and the shelves and the mighty table. For oak was, and will be again, the chief wood of the weald.

When they put food and ale before me, it was of the kind which has been English ever since England began, and which perhaps good fortune will preserve over the breakdown of our generation, until we have England back again. One could see the hops in the tankard, and one could taste the barley, until, more and more sunk into the plenitude of this good house, one could dare to contemplate, as though from a distant standpoint, the corruption and the imminent danger of the time through which we must lead our lives. And, as I so considered the ruin of the great cities and their slime, I felt as though I were in a fortress of virtue and of health, which could hold out through the pressure of the war. And I thought to myself: " Perhaps even before our children are men, these parts which survive from a better order will be accepted as models, and England will be built again."

This fantasy had not time, tenuous as it was, to disappear, before there came into that room a man whose gesture and bearing promised him to be an excellent companion, but in whose eyes I also perceived some light not ordinary. He was of middle age, fifty or more; his hair was crisp and grey, his face brown, as though he had been much upon the sea. He was tall in stature, and of some strength. He saluted me, and, when he had eaten, asked me if I also were familiar with this inn.

"Very familiar," I said; "and since I can enter it at any hour freely, it is now more familiar to me even than the houses that were once my homes. For nowadays we, who work in the State and are not idle, must be driven from one place to another; and only the very rich have certitude and continuity. But to them it is of no service; for they are too idle to take root in the soil."

"Yet I was of their blood," he said; "and there is in this county a home which should be mine. But nothing to-day is capable of endurance. I have not seen my home (though it is but ten miles from here) since I left it in my thirtieth year; and I too would rather come to this inn, which I know as you know it, than to any house in England; because I am certain of entry, and because I know what I shall find, and because what I find is what any man of this county should find, if the soul of it is not to disappear."

"You, then," I answered (we were now seated side by side before the fire with but one flickering candle behind us, and on the floor between us a port just younger than the host), "you, then, come here for much the same reason as do I?"

"And what is that?" said he.

"Why," said I, "to enjoy the illusion that Change can somewhere be arrested, and that, in some shape, a part at least of the things we love remains. For, since I was a boy and almost since I can remember, everything in this house has been the same; and here I escape from the threats of the society we know."

When I had said this, he was grave and silent for a little while; and then he answered:

"It is impossible, I think, after many years to recover any such illusion. Just as a young man can no longer think himself (as children do) the actor in any drama of his own choosing, so a man growing old (as am I) can no longer expect of any society — and least of all of his own — the gladness that comes from an illusion of permanence."

" For my part," I answered in turn,
" I know very well, though I can con-
jure up this feeling of security, that
it is very flimsy stuff; and I take it
rather as men take symbols. For
though these good people will at last
perish, and some brewer — a Colonel
of Volunteers as like as not — will buy
this little field, and though for the port
we are drinking there will be imperial
port, and for the beer we have just
drunk something as noisome as that
port, and though thistles will grow
up in the good pasture ground, and
though, in a word, this inn will become
a hotel and will perish, nevertheless
I cannot but believe that England
remains, and I do not think it the taking of a drug or a deliberate cheating
of oneself to come and steep one's soul
in what has already endured so long
because it was proper to our country."

"All that you say," he answered, "is but part of the attempt to escape Necessity. Your very frame is of that substance for which permanence means death; and every one of all the emotions that you know is of its nature momentary, and must be so if it is to be alive."

"Yet there is a divine thirst," I said, "for something that will not so perish. If there were no such thirst, why should you and I debate such things, or come here to The Lion either of us, to taste antiquity? And if that thirst is there, it is a proof that there is for us some End and some such satisfaction. For my part, as I know of nothing else, I cannot but seek it in this visible good world. I seek it in Sussex, in the nature of my home, and in the tradition of my blood."

But he answered: "No; it is not

thus to be attained, the end of which you speak. And that thirst, which surely is divine, is to be quenched in no stream that we can find by journeying, not even in the little rivers that run here under the combes of home."

MYSELF : "Well, then, what is the End ?"

HE: "I have sometimes seen it clearly, that when the disappointed quest was over, all this journeying would turn out to be but the beginning of a much greater adventure, and that I should set out towards another place where every sense should be fulfilled, and where the fear of mutation should be set at rest."

MYSELF : "No one denies that such a picture in the mind haunts men their whole lives through, though, after they have once experienced loss and incompletion, and especially when they have caught sight a long way off of the Barrier which ends all our experience, they recognise that picture for a cheat; and surely nothing can save it? That which reasons in us may be absolute and undying; for it is outside Time. It escapes the gropings of the learned, and it has nothing to do with material things. But as for all those functions which we but half fulfil in life, surely elsewhere they cannot be fulfilled at all? Colour is for the eyes and music is for the ears; and all that we love so much comes in by channels that do not remain."

HE: "Yet the Desire can only be for things that we have known; and the Desire, as you have said, is a proof of the thing desired, and, but for these things which we know, the words 'joy' and 'contentment' and 'fulfilment' would have no meaning."

MYSELF: "Why yes; but, though desires are the strongest evidence of truth, yet there is also desire for illusions, as there is a waking demand for things attainable, and a demand in dreams for things fantastic and unreal. Every analogy increasingly persuades us, and so does the whole scheme of things as we learn it, that, with our passing, there shall also pass speech and comfortable fires and fields and the voices of our children, and that, when they pass, we lose them for ever."

HE: "Yet these things would not be, but for the mind which receives them; and how can we make sure what channels are necessary for the mind? and may not the mind stretch on? And you, since you reject my guess at what may be reserved for us, tell me, what is the End which we shall attain?"

MYSELF : " *Salva fide,* I cannot tell."

Then he continued and said : " I have too long considered these matters for any opposition between one experience and another to affect my spirit, and I know that a long and careful inquiry into any matter must lead the same man to opposing conclusions ; but, for my part, I shall confidently expect throughout that old age, which is not far from me, that, when it ceases, I shall find beyond it things similar to those which I have known.   For all I here enjoy is of one nature ; and if the life of a man be bereft of them at last, then it is falsehood or metaphor to use the word ' eternal.' "

" You think, then," said I, " that some immortal part in us is concerned not only with our knowledge, but with our every feeling, and that our final satisfaction will include a sensual pleasure : fragrance, and landscape, and a visible home that shall be dearer even than these dear hills ? ”

“ Something of the sort,” he said, and slightly shrugged his shoulders. They were broad, as he sat beside me staring at the fire. They conveyed in their attitude that effect of mingled strength and weariness which is common to all who have travelled far and with great purpose, perpetually seeking some worthy thing which they could never find.

The fire had fallen. Flames no longer leapt from the beech logs ; but on their under side, where a glow still lingered, embers fell.

THE AUTUMN AND THE FALL
OF LEAVES

IT is not true that the close of a life
which ends in a natural fashion—
life which is permitted to put on the
pomp of death and to go out in glory
— inclines the mind to repose. It is
not true of a day ending nor the passing of the year, nor of the fall of leaves.
Whatever permanent, uneasy question
is native to men, comes forward most
insistent and most loud at such times.

There is a house in my own county
which is built of stone, whose gardens
are fitted to the autumn. It has level
alleys standing high and banked with
stone. Their ornaments were carved
under the influence of that restraint
which marked the Stuarts. They
stand above old ponds, and are strewn
at this moment with the leaves of elms.

These walks are like the Mailles of the Flemish cities, the walls of the French towns or the terraces of the Loire. They are enjoyed to-day by whoever has seen all our time go racing by; they are the proper resting-places of the aged, and their spirit is felt especially in the fall of leaves.

At this season a sky which is of so delicate and faint a blue as to contain something of gentle mockery, and certainly more of tenderness, presides at the fall of leaves. There is no air, no breath at all. The leaves are so light that they sidle on their going downward, hesitating in that which is not void to them, and touching at last so imperceptibly the earth with which they are to mingle, that the gesture is much gentler than a salutation, and even more discreet than a discreet caress.

They make a little sound, less than the least of sounds. No bird at night in the marshes rustles so slightly; no man, though men are the subtlest of living beings, puts so evanescent a stress upon their sacred whispers or their prayers. The leaves are hardly heard, but they are heard just so much that men also, who are destined at the end to grow glorious and to die, look up and hear them falling.

.   .   .   .

With what a pageantry of every sort is not that troubling symbol surrounded! The scent of life is never fuller in the woods than now, for the ground is yielding up its memories. The spring when it comes will not restore this fullness, nor these deep and ample recollections of the earth. For the earth seems now to remember

the drive of the ploughshare and its
harrying; the seed, and the full burst-
ing of it, the swelling and the comple-
tion of the harvest. Up to the edge
of the woods throughout the weald the
earth has borne fruit; the barns are
full, and the wheat is standing stacked
in the fields, and there are orchards
all around. It is upon such a mood
of parentage and of fruition that the
dead leaves fall.

The colour is not a mere splendour:
it is intricate. The same unbounded
power, never at fault and never in
calculation, which comprehends all
the landscapé, and which has made
the woods, has worked in each one
separate leaf as well; they are incon-
ceivably varied. Take up one leaf
and see. How many kinds of bound-
ary are there here between the stain
which ends in a sharp edge against

the gold, and the sweep in which the purple and red mingle more evenly than they do in shot-silk or in flames? Nor are the boundaries to be measured only by degrees of definition. They have also their characters of line. Here in this leaf are boundaries intermittent, boundaries rugged, boundaries curved, and boundaries broken. Nor do shape and definition ever begin to exhaust the list. For there are softness and hardness too: the agreement and disagreement with the scheme of veins; the grotesque and the simple in line; the sharp and the broad, the smooth, and raised in boundaries. So in this one matter of boundaries might you discover for ever new things; there is no end to them. Their qualities are infinite. And beside boundaries you have hues and tints, shades also, varying thicknesses of stuff, and endless choice of surface; that list also is infinite, and the divisions of each item in it are infinite; nor is it of any use to analyse the thing, for everywhere the depth and the meaning of so much creation are beyond our powers. And all this is true of but one dead leaf; and yet every dead leaf will differ from its fellow.

That which has delighted to excel in boundlessness within the bounds of this one leaf, has also transformed the whole forest. There is no number to the particular colour of the one leaf. The forest is like a thing so changeful of its nature that change clings to it as a quality, apparent even during the glance of a moment. This forest makes a picture which is designed, but not seizable. It is a scheme, but a scheme you cannot set down. It is of those things which can best be retained by mere copying with a pencil or a brush. It is of those things which a man cannot fully receive, and which he cannot fully re-express to other men.

It is no wonder, then, that at this peculiar time, this week (or moment) of the year, the desires which if they do not prove at least demand — perhaps remember — our destiny, come strongest. They are proper to the time of autumn, and all men feel them. The air is at once new and old; the morning (if one rises early enough to welcome its leisurely advance) contains something in it of profound reminiscence. The evenings hardly yet suggest (as they soon will) friends and security, and the fires of home. The thoughts awakened in us by their bands of light fading along the downs are thoughts which go with loneliness and prepare me for the isolation of the soul.

It is on this account that tradition has set, at the entering of autumn, for a watch at the gate of the season, the Archangel; and at its close the day and the night of All-Hallows on which the dead return.

ON SACRAMENTAL THINGS

IT is good for a man's soul to sit
down in the silence by himself and
to think of those things which happen
by some accident to be in communion
with the whole world.   If he has not
the faculty of remembering these
things in their order and of calling
them up one after another in his mind,
then let him write them down as they
come to him upon a piece of paper.
They will comfort him ; they will prove
a sort of solace against the expecta-
tion of the end.   To consider such
things is a sacramental occupation.
And yet the more I think of them the
less I can quite understand in what
elements their power consists.

A woman smiling at a little child,
not knowing that others see her, and

holding out her hands towards it, and in one of her hands flowers; an old man, lean and active, with an eager face, walking at dusk upon a warm and windy evening westward towards a clear sunset below dark and flying clouds; a group of soldiers, seen suddenly in manœuvres, each man intent upon his business, all working at the wonderful trade, taking their places with exactitude and order and yet with elasticity; a deep, strong tide running back to the sea, going noiselessly and flat and black and smooth, and heavy with purpose under an old wall; the sea smell of a Channel seaport town; a ship coming up at one out of the whole sea when one is in a little boat and is waiting for her, coming up at one with her great sails merry and every one doing its work, with the life of the wind in her, and a balance, rhythm, and give in all that she does which marries her to the sea — whether it be a fore and aft rig and one sees only great lines of the white, or a square rig and one sees what is commonly and well called a leaning tower of canvas, or that primal rig, the triangular sail, that cuts through the airs of the world and clove a way for the first adventures, whatever its rig, a ship so approaching an awaiting boat from which we watch her is one of the things I mean.

I would that the taste of my time permitted a lengthy list of such things : they are pleasant to remember ! They do so nourish the mind ! A glance of sudden comprehension mixed with mercy and humour from the face of a lover or a friend ; the noise of wheels when the guns are going by ; the clatter-clank-clank of the pieces and the shouted halt at the head of the column; the noise of many horses, the metallic but united and harmonious clamour of all those ironed hoofs, rapidly occupying the highway; chief and most persistent memory, a great hill when the morning strikes it and one sees it up before one round the turning of a rock after the long passes and despairs of the night.

When a man has journeyed and journeyed through those hours in which there is no colour or shape, all along the little hours that were made for sleep and when, therefore, the waking soul is bewildered or despairs, the morning is always a resurrection —but especially when it reveals a height in the sky.

This last picture I would particularly cherish, so great a consolation is it, and so permanent a grace does it lend later to the burdened mind of a man.

For when a man looks back upon his many journeys — so many rivers crossed, and more than one of them forded in peril; so many swinging mountain roads, so many difficult steeps and such long wastes of plains — of all the pictures that impress themselves by the art or kindness of whatever god presides over the success of journeys, no picture more remains than that picture of a great hill when the day first strikes it after the long burden of the night.

Whatever reasons a man may have for occupying the darkness with his travel and his weariness, those reasons must be out of the ordinary and must go with some bad strain upon the mind. Perhaps one undertook the march from an evil necessity under

the coercion of other men, or perhaps
in terror, hoping that the darkness
might hide one, or perhaps for cool,
dreading the unnatural heat of noon
in a desert land; perhaps haste, which
is in itself so wearying a thing, com-
pelled one, or perhaps anxiety. Or
perhaps, most dreadful of all, one hur-
ried through the night afoot because
one feared what otherwise the night
would bring, a night empty of sleep
and a night whose dreams were waking dreams and evil.

But whatever prompts the adventure or the necessity, when the long
burden has been borne, and when the
turn of the hours has come; when the
stars have grown paler; when colour
creeps back greyly and uncertainly to
the earth, first into the greens of the
high pastures, then here and there
upon a rock or a pool with reeds,

while all the air, still cold, is full of
the scent of morning; while one
notices the imperceptible disappear-
ance of the severities of Heaven until
at last only the morning star hangs
splendid; when in the end of that
miracle the landscape is fully revealed,
and one finds into what country one
has come; then a great hill before
one, losing the forests upwards into
rock and steep meadow upon its sides,
and towering at last into the peaks
and crests of the inaccessible places,
gives a soul to the new land. . . .
The sun, in a single moment and with
the immediate summons of a trumpet-
call, strikes the spear-head of the high
places, and at once the valley, though
still in shadow, is transfigured, and
with the daylight all manner of things
have come back to the world.

Hope is the word which gathers the

origins of those things together, and
hope is the seed of what they mean,
but that new light and its new quality
is more than hope. Livelihood is
come back with the sunrise, and the
fixed certitude of the soul; number
and measure and comprehension have
returned, and a just appreciation of
all reality is the gift of the new day.
Glory (which, if men would only know
it, lies behind all true certitude) illu-
mines and enlivens the seen world,
and the living light makes of the true
things now revealed something more
than truth absolute; they appear as
truth acting and creative.

This first shaft of the sun is to that
hill and valley what a word is to a
thought. It is to that hill and valley
what verse is to the common story
told; it is to that hill and valley what
music is to verse. And there lies

behind it, one is very sure, an infinite
progress of such exaltations, so that
one begins to understand, as the pure
light shines and grows and as the
limit of shadow descends the vast
shoulder of the steep, what has been
meant by those great phrases which
still lead on, still comfort, and still
make darkly wise, the uncomforted
wondering of mankind. Such is the
famous phrase : " Eye has not seen
nor ear heard, nor can it enter into the
heart of man what things God has prepared for those that serve Him."

So much, then, is conveyed by a
hill-top at sunrise when it comes upon
the traveller or the soldier after the
long march of a night, the bending
of the shoulders, and the emptiness of
the dark.

Many other things put one into communion with the whole world.

Who does not remember coming over a lifting road to a place where the ridge is topped, and where, upon the further side, a broad landscape, novel or endeared by memory (for either is a good thing), bursts upon the seized imagination as a wave from the open sea, swelling up an inland creek, breaks and bursts upon the rocks of the shore? There is a place where a man passes from the main valley of the Rhone over into the valley of the Isère, and where the Gresivandan so suddenly comes upon him. Two gates of limestone rock, high as the first shoulders of the mountains, lead into the valley which they guard; it is a province of itself, a level floor of thirty miles, nourished by one river, and walled in up to the clouds on either side.

Or, again, in the champagne country,

moving between great blocks of wood in the Forest of Rheims and always going upward as the ride leads him, a man comes to a point whence he suddenly sees all that vast plain of the invasions stretching out to where, very far off against the horizon, two days away, twin summits mark the whole site sharply with a limit as a frame marks a picture or a punctuation a phrase.

There is another place more dear to me, but which I doubt whether any other but a native of that place can know. After passing through the plough lands of an empty plateau, a traveller breaks through a little fringe of chestnut hedge and perceives at once before him the wealthiest and the most historical of European things, the chief of the great capitals of Christendom and the arena in which is now debated (and has been for how long!) the Faith, the chief problem of this world.

Apart from landscape other things belong to this contemplation: Notes of music, and, stronger even than repeated and simple notes of music, a subtle scent and its association, a familiar printed page. Perhaps the test of these sacramental things is their power to revive the past.

There is a story translated into the noblest of English writing by Dasent. It is to be found in his "Tales from the Norse." It is called the Story of the Master Maid.

A man had found in his youth a woman on the Norwegian hills: this woman was faëry, and there was a spell upon her. But he won her out of it in various ways, and they crossed the sea together, and he would bring her to his father's house, but his father was a King. As they went over-sea together alone, he said and swore to her that he would never forget how they had met and loved each other without warning, but by an act of God, upon the Dovrefjeld. Come near his father's house, the ordinary influences of the ordinary day touched him; he bade her enter a hut and wait a moment until he had warned his father of so strange a marriage; she, however, gazing into his eyes, and knowing how the divine may be transformed into the earthly, quite as surely as the earthly into the divine, makes him promise that he will not eat human food. He sits at his father's table, still steeped in her and in the seas. He forgets his vow and eats human food, and at once he forgets.

Then follows much for which I have

not space, but the woman in the hut by her magic causes herself to be at last sent for to the father's palace. The young man sees her, and is only slightly troubled as by a memory which he cannot grasp. They talk together as strangers; but looking out of the window by accident the King's son sees a bird and its mate; he points them out to the woman, and she says suddenly: "So was it with you and me high up upon the Dovrefjeld." Then he remembers all.

Now that story is a symbol, and tells the truth. We see some one thing in this world, and suddenly it becomes particular and sacramental; a woman and a child, a man at evening, a troop of soldiers; we hear notes of music, we smell the smell that went with a passed time, or we discover after the long night a shaft of light upon the tops of the hills at morning: there is a resurrection, and we are refreshed and renewed.

But why all these things are so neither I nor any other man can tell.

ON REST

THERE was a priest once who
preached a sermon to the text
of "Abba, Father." On that text one
might preach anything, but the matter
that he chose was "Rest." He was
not yet in middle age, and those who
heard him were not yet even young.
They could not understand at all the
moment of his ardent speech, and even
the older men, seeing him to be but
in the central part of life, wondered
that he should speak so. His eyes
were illuminated by the vision of
something distant; his heart was not
ill at ease, but, as it were, fixedly
expectant, and he preached from his
little pulpit in that little chapel of the
Downs, with rising and deeper powers
of the voice, so that he shook the air;

yet all this energy was but the praise or the demand for the surcease of energy, and all this sound was but the demand for silence.

It is a thing, I say, incomprehensible to the young, but gradually comprehended as the years go droning by, that in all things (and in proportion to the intensity of the life of each) there comes this appetite for dissolution and for repose : I do not mean that repose beyond which further effort is demanded, but something final and supreme.

This priest, a year or so after he had appealed with his sermon before that little country audience in the emptiness of the Downs, died. He had that which he desired, Rest. But what is it ? What is the nature of this thing ?

Note you how great soldiers, when

their long campaigns are done, are
indifferent to further wars, and look
largely upon the nature of fighting
men, their objects, their failures, their
victories, their rallying, their momentary cheers. Not that they grow indifferent to that great trade which is the
chief business of a State, the defence
or the extension of the common weal ;
but that after so much expense of all
the senses our God gave them, a sort
of charity and justice fills their minds.
I have often remarked how men who
had most lost and won, even in arms,
would turn the leisured part of their
lives to the study of the details of
struggle, and seemed equally content
to be describing the noble fortunes of
an army, whether it were upon the crest
of advancing victory, or in the agony
of a surrender. This was because the
the writers had found Rest. And

throughout the history of Letters —
of Civilisation, and of contemporary
friends, one may say that in proportion to the largeness of their action is
this largeness and security of vision
at the end.

Now, note another thing: that, when
we speak of an end, by that very word
we mean two things. For first we
mean the cessation of Form, and perhaps of Idea; but also we mean a
goal, or object, to which the Form and
the Idea perpetually tended, without
which they would have had neither
meaning nor existence, and in which
they were at last fulfilled. Aristotle
could give no summing up but this to
all his philosophy, that there was a
nature, not only of all, but of each,
and that the end determined what
that nature might be; which is also
what we Christians mean when we say

that God made the world; and great Rabelais, when his great books were ending, could but conclude that all things tended to their end. Tennyson also, before he died, having written for so many years a poetry which one must be excused in believing considerable, felt, as how many have felt it, the thrumming of the ebb tide when the sea calls back the feudal allegiance of the rivers. I know it upon Arun bar. The Flood, when the sea heaves up and pours itself into the inland channels, bears itself creatively, and is like the manhood of a man — first tentative, then gathering itself for action, then sweeping suddenly at the charge. It carries with it the wind from the open horizon, it determines suddenly, it spurs, and sweeps, and is victorious; the current races; the harbour is immediately full.

But the ebb tide is of another kind. With a long, slow power, whose motive is at once downward steadily towards its authority and its obedience and desire, it pushes as with shoulders, home ; and for many hours the stream goes darkly, swiftly, and steadily. It is intent, direct, and level. It is a thing for evenings, and it is under an evening when there is little wind, that you may best observe the symbol thus presented by material things. For everything in nature has in it something sacramental, teaching the soul of man ; and nothing more possesses that high quality than the motion of a river when it meets the sea. The water at last hangs dully, the work is done ; and those who have permitted the lesson to instruct their minds are aware of consummation.

Men living in cities have often

wondered how it was that the men in the open who knew horses and the earth or ships and the salt water risk so much — and for what reward? It is an error in the very question they ask, rather than in the logical puzzle they approach, which falsifies their wonder. There is no reward. To die in battle, to break one's neck at a hedge, to sink or to be swamped are not rewards. But action demands an end; there is a fruit to things; and everything we do (here at least, and within the bonds of time) may not exceed the little limits of a nature which it neither made nor acquired for itself, but was granted.

Some say that old men fear death. It is the theme of the debased and the vulgar. It is not true. Those who have imperfectly served are ready enough; those who have served more perfectly are glad — as though there stood before them a natural transition and a condition of their being.

So it says in a book "all good endings are but shining transitions." And, again, there is a sonnet which says:

We will not whisper: we have found the place
  Of silence and the ancient halls of sleep,
  And that which breathes alone throughout the deep
The end and the beginning; and the face
Between the level brows of whose blind eyes
  Lie plenary contentment, full surcease
  Of violence, and the ultimate great peace
Wherein we lose our human lullabies.

Look up and tell the immeasurable height
  Between the vault of the world and your dear head;
That 's Death, my little sister, and the Night
  That was our Mother beckons us to bed:
Where large oblivion in her house is laid
For us tired children now our games are played.

Indeed, one might quote the poets (who are the teachers of mankind) indefinitely in this regard. They are all agreed. What did Sleep and Death to the body of Sarpedon? They took it home. And every one who dies in all the Epics is better for the dying. Some complain of it afterwards I will admit; but they are hard to please. Roland took it as the end of battle; and there was a Scandinavian fellow caught on the north-east coast, I think, who in dying thanked God for all the joy he had had in his life — as you may have heard before. And St. Anthony of Assisi (not of Padua) said, " Welcome, little sister Death! " as was his way. And one who stands right up above most men who write or speak said it was the only port after the tide-streams and bar-handling of this journey.

So it is; let us be off to the hills. The silence and the immensity that inhabit them are the simulacra of such things.

ON COMING TO AN END

OF all the simple actions in the world! Of all the simple actions in the world!

One would think it could be done with less effort than the heaving of a sigh. . . . Well — then, one would be wrong.

There is no case of Coming to an End but has about it something of an effort and a jerk, as though Nature abhorred it, and though it be true that some achieve a quiet and a perfect end to one thing or another (as, for instance, to Life), yet this achievement is not arrived at save through the utmost toil, and consequent upon the most persevering and exquisite art.

Now you can say that this may be

true of sentient things but not of things inanimate. It is true even of things inanimate.

Look down some straight railway line for a vanishing point to the perspective : you will never find it. Or try to mark the moment when a small target becomes invisible. There is no gradation ; a moment it was there, and you missed it — possibly because the Authorities were not going in for journalism that day, and had not chosen a dead calm with the light full on the canvas. A moment it was there and then, as you steamed on, it was gone. The same is true of a lark in the air. You see it and then you do not see it, you only hear its song. And the same is true of that song : you hear it and then suddenly you do not hear it. It is true of a human voice, which is familiar in your ear, living and inhabiting the rooms of your house. There comes a day when it ceases altogether — and how positive, how definite and hard is that Coming to an End.

It does not leave an echo behind it, but a sharp edge of emptiness, and very often as one sits beside the fire the memory of that voice suddenly returning gives to the silence about one a personal force, as it were, of obsession and of control. So much happens when even one of all our million voices Comes to an End.

It is necessary, it is august and it is reasonable that the great story of our lives also should be accomplished and should reach a term : and yet there is something in that hidden duality of ours which makes the prospect of so natural a conclusion terrible, and it is the better judgment of mankind and the mature conclusion of civilisations in their age that there is not only a conclusion here but something of an adventure also. It may be so.

Those who solace mankind and are the principal benefactors of it, I mean the poets and the musicians, have attempted always to ease the prospect of Coming to an End, whether it were the Coming to an End of the things we love or of that daily habit and conversation which is our life and is the atmosphere wherein we loved them. Indeed this is a clear test whereby you may distinguish the great artists from the mean hucksters and charlatans, that the first approach and reveal what is dreadful with calm and, as it were, with a purpose to use it for good while the vulgar catchpenny fellows must liven up their bad dishes as with a cheap sauce of the horrible, caring nothing, so that their shrieks sell, whether we are the better for them or no.

The great poets, I say, bring us easily or grandly to the gate: as in that *Ode to a Nightingale* where it is thought good (in an immortal phrase) to pass painlessly at midnight, or, in the glorious line which Ronsard uses, like a salute with the sword, hailing " la profitable mort."

The noblest or the most perfect of English elegies leaves, as a sort of savour after the reading of it, no terror at all nor even too much regret, but the landscape of England at evening, when the smoke of the cottages mixes with autumn vapours among the elms; and even that gloomy modern *Ode to the West Wind*, unfinished and touched with despair, though it will speak of —

> . . . . that outer place forlorn
> Which, like an infinite grey sea, surrounds
> With everlasting calm the land of human sounds ;

yet also returns to the sacramental earth of one's childhood where it says :

> For now the Night completed tells her tale
> Of rest and dissolution : gathering round
> Her mist in such persuasion that the ground
>   Of Home consents to falter and grow pale.
>   And the stars are put out and the trees fail.
> Nor anything remains but that which drones
> Enormous through the dark. . . .

And again, in another place, where it prays that one may at the last be fed with beauty —

> . . . . as the flowers are fed
> That fill their falling-time with generous breath :
> Let me attain a natural end of death,
>   And on the mighty breast, as on a bed,
>   Lay decently at last a drowsy head,
> Content to lapse in somnolence and fade
> In dreaming once again the dream of all things made.

The most careful philosophy, the most heavenly music, the best choice

of poetic or prosaic phrase prepare
men properly for man's perpetual loss
of this and of that, and introduce us
proudly to the similar and greater
business of departure from them all,
from whatever of them all remains at
the close.

To be introduced, to be prepared,
to be armoured, all these are excellent things, but there is a question no
foresight can answer nor any comprehension resolve. It is right to gather
upon that question the varied affec-
tions or perceptions of varying men.

I knew a man once in the Tourde-
noise, a gloomy man, but very rich,
who cared little for the things he
knew. This man took no pleasure in
his fruitful orchards and his carefully
ploughed fields and his harvests. He
took pleasure in pine trees; he was a
man of groves and of the dark. For

him that things should come to an end
was but part of an universal rhythm ;
a part pleasing to the general har-
mony, and making in the music of the
world about him a solemn and, oh, a
conclusive chord. This man would
study the sky at night and take from
it a larger and a larger draught of infin-
itude, finding in this exercise not a
mere satisfaction, but an object and
goal for the mind ; when he had so
wandered for a while under the night
he seemed, for the moment, to have
reached the object of his being.

And I knew another man in the
Weald who worked with his hands,
and was always kind, and knew his
trade well ; he smiled when he talked
of scythes, and he could thatch. He
could fish also, and he knew about
grafting, and about the seasons of
plants, and birds, and the way of seed.

He had a face full of weather, he fatigued his body, he watched his land. He would not talk much of mysteries, he would rather hum songs. He loved new friends and old. He had lived with one wife for fifty years, and he had five children, who were a policeman, a schoolmistress, a son at home, and two who were sailors. This man said that what a man did and the life in which he did it was like the farmwork upon a summer's day. He said one works a little and rests, and works a little again, and one drinks, and there is a perpetual talk with those about one. Then (he would say) the shadows lengthen at evening, the wind falls, the birds get back home. And as for ourselves, we are sleepy before it is dark.

Then also I knew a third man who lived in a town and was clerical and did no work, for he had money of his own. This man said that all we do and the time in which we do it is rather a night than a day. He said that when we came to an end we vanished, we and our works, but that we vanished into a broadening light.

Which of these three knew best the nature of man and of his works, and which knew best of what nature was the end?

.   .   .   .

Why so glum, my Lad, or my Lass (as the case may be), why so heavy at heart? Did you not know that you also must Come to an End?

Why, that woman of Etaples who sold such Southern wine for the dissipation of the Picardian Mist, her time is over and gone and the wine has been drunk long ago and the singers in her house have departed, and the wind of the sea moans in and fills their hall. The Lords who died in Roncesvalles have been dead these thousand years and more, and the loud song about them grew very faint and dwindled and is silent now: there is nothing at all remains.

It is certain that the hills decay and that rivers as the dusty years proceed run feebly and lose themselves at last in desert sands; and in its æons the very firmament grows old. But evil also is perishable and bad men meet their judge. Be comforted.

Now of all endings, of all Comings to an End none is so hesitating as the ending of a book which the Publisher will have so long and the writer so short: and the Public (God Bless the Public) will have whatever it is given.

Books, however much their lingering, books also must Come to an End. It is abhorrent to their nature as to the life of man. They must be sharply cut off. Let it be done at once and fixed as by a spell and the power of a Word; the word FINIS.